YOUR Godmother's LOVE

A Heartfelt Keepsake Story Book for A New Baby and Their Godmother

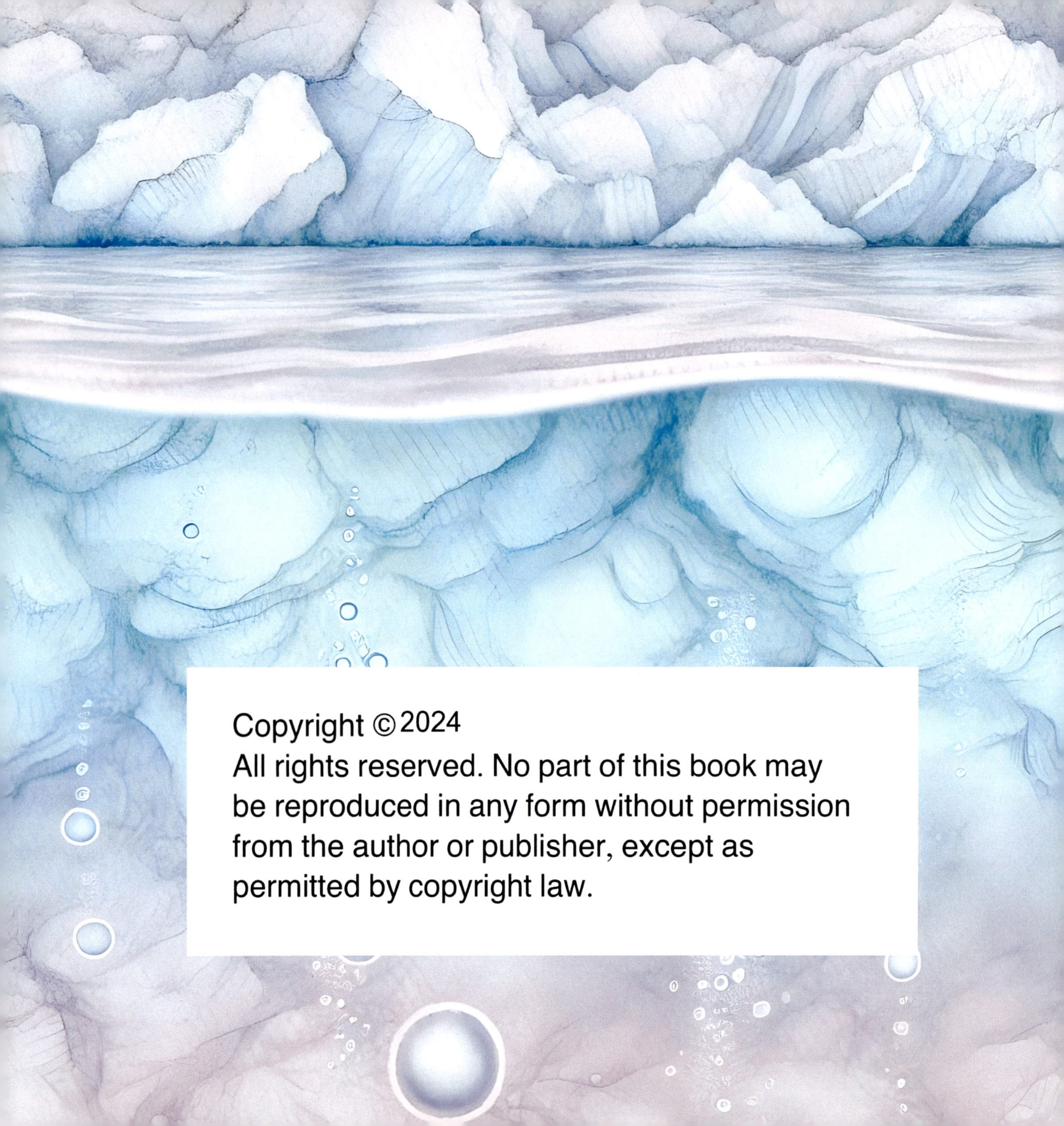

Your Godmother's love is
unlike any other
It's special and unwavering,
we have faith in each other.
I'll be by your side
through sunshine and rain.
Guide you in joy and hold you
through pain.
This bond we share,
forever will stay
A light on your journey,
come what may.

In every sunrise,
find the light.
Keep courage close
and hold your dreams
tight.

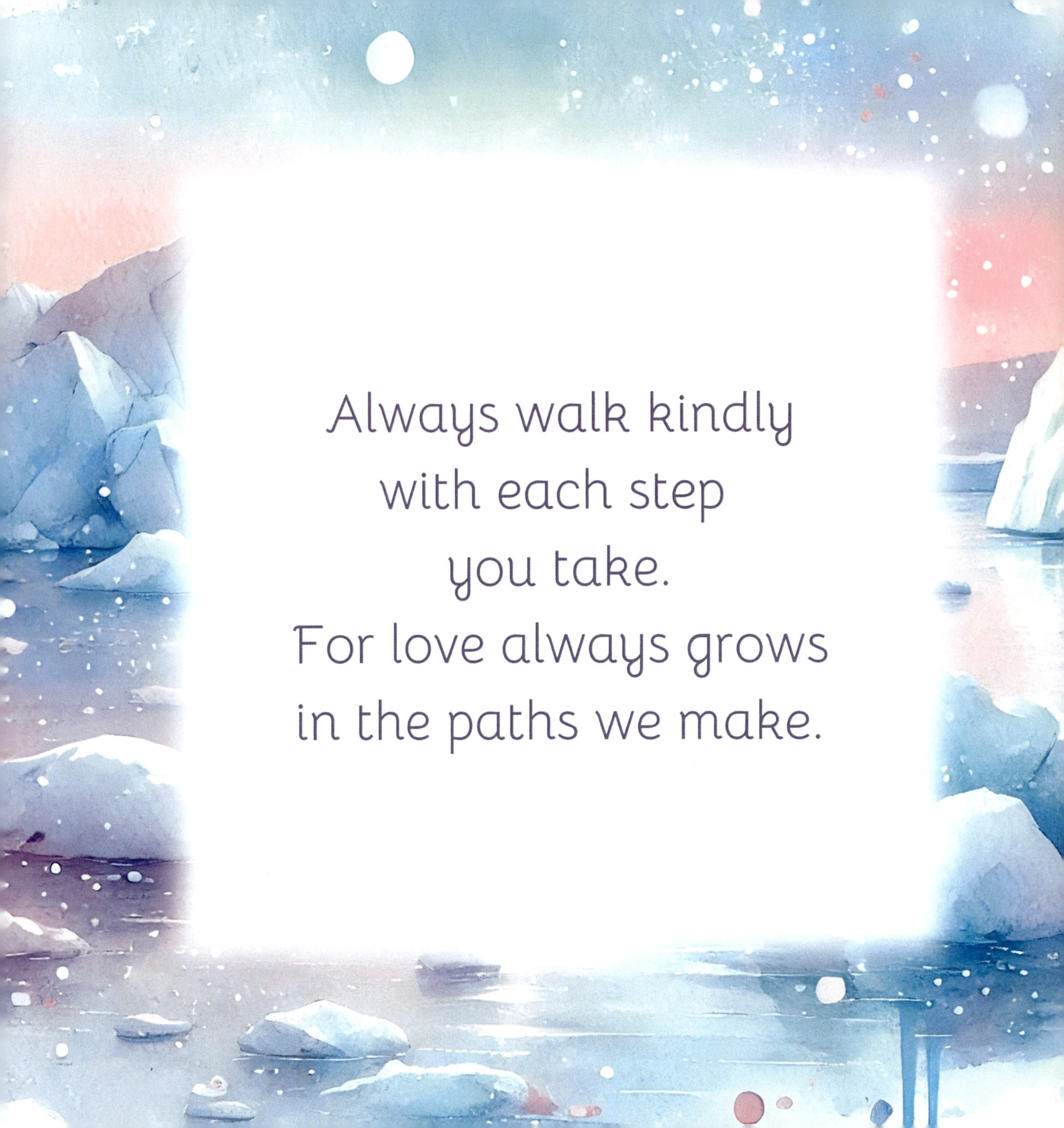

Always walk kindly
with each step
you take.
For love always grows
in the paths we make.

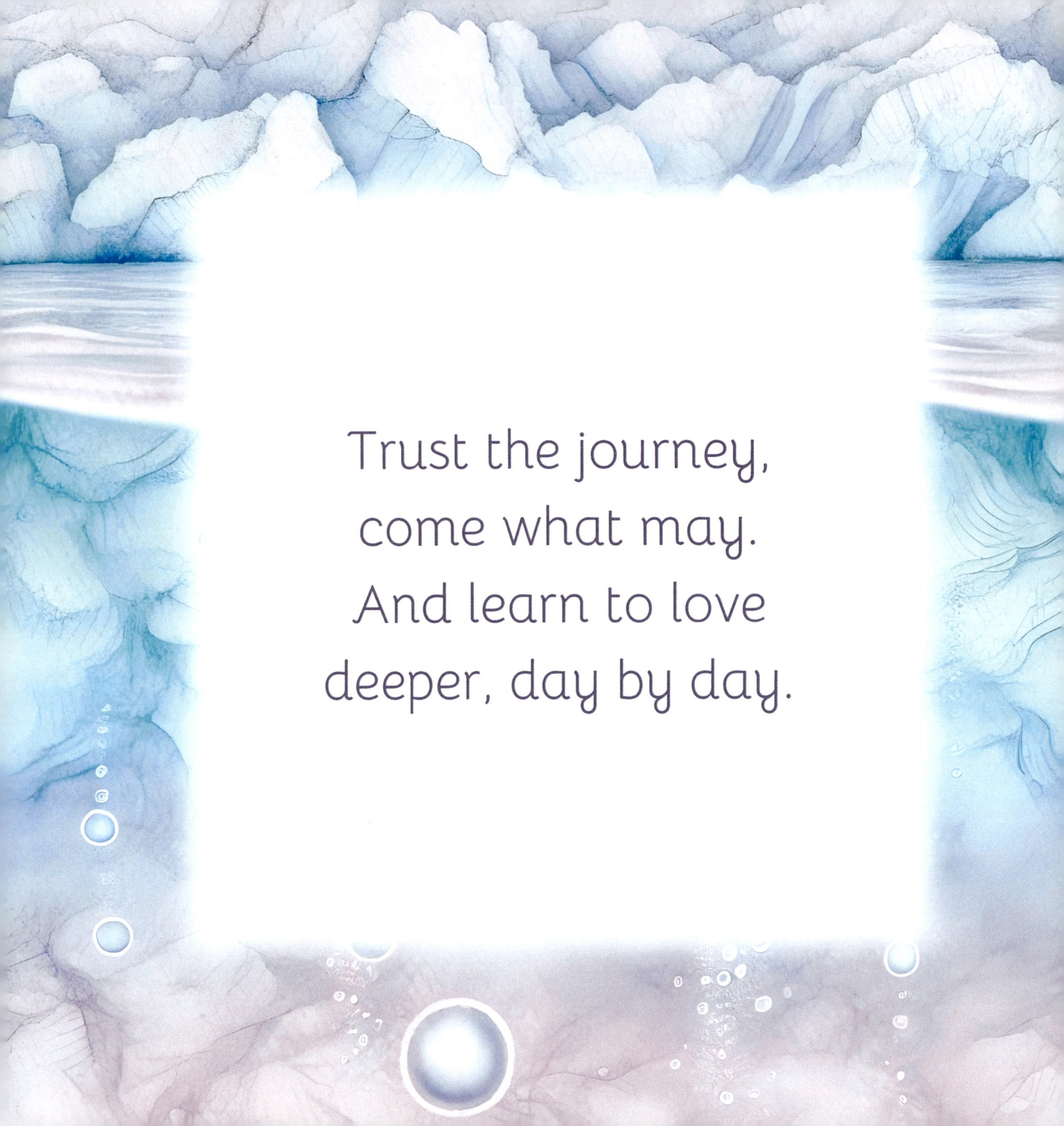

Trust the journey,
come what may.
And learn to love
deeper, day by day.

Know that the lord is
your steady guide.
But when you need me,
I'll be by your side.

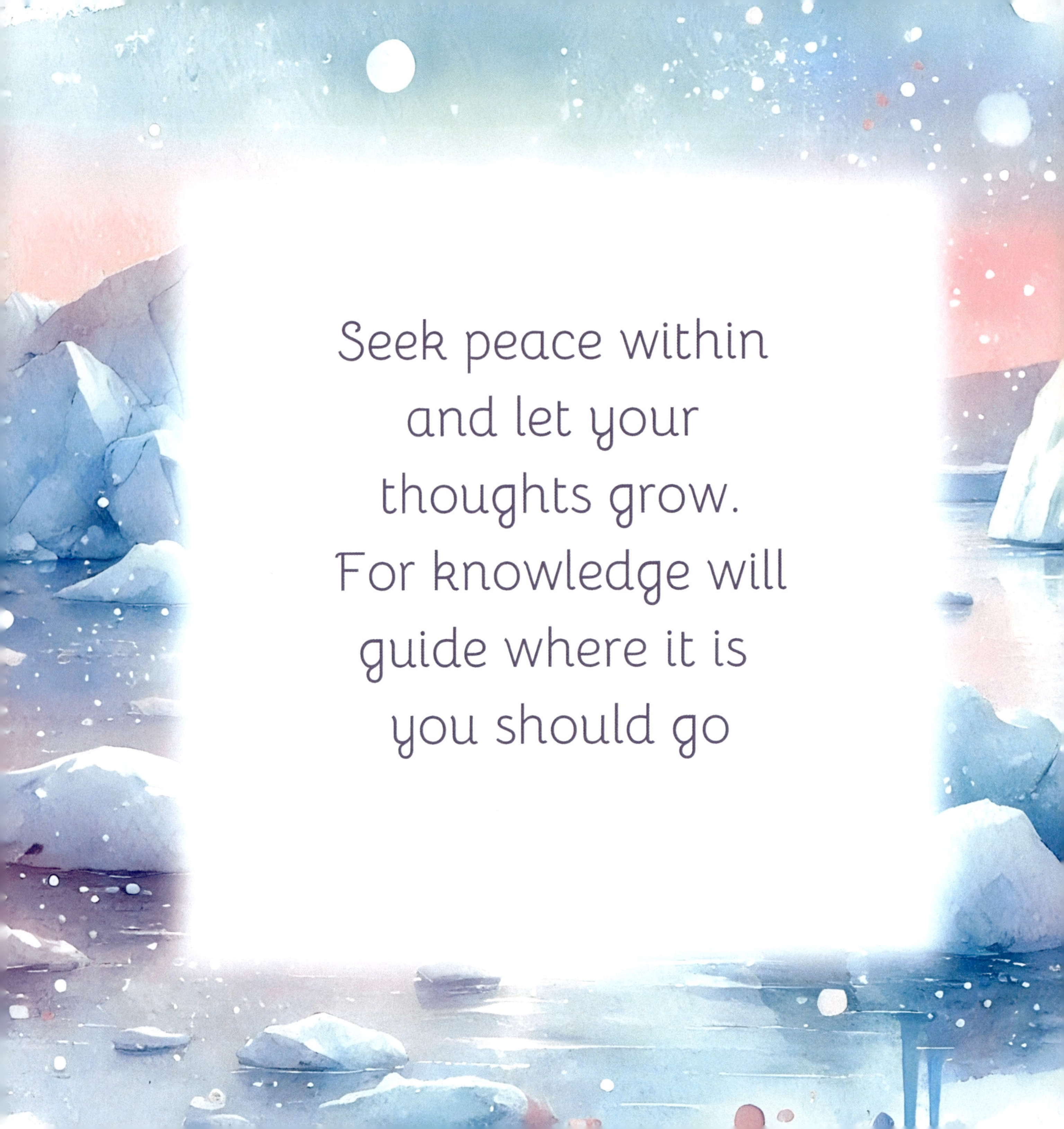

Seek peace within
and let your
thoughts grow.
For knowledge will
guide where it is
you should go

Have love for your
neighbour,
both near and far.
God's grace will shine
brighter than
any star.

When storms arrive,
as storms always do.
Stand tall, be proud
and let your heart
stay true.

Always speak with
grace and let
kindness lead.
Your faith will grow
stronger indeed.

In giving you will
always find joy anew.
The world will grow
richer through you too!

When lost or weary,
don't despair.
Know that each night
heaven hears your
prayer.

Be thankful child, for
each small grace.
For it's through simple
blessings that we find
our place.

Hold onto your hope,
even when small.
It will always shine
brightly through it all.

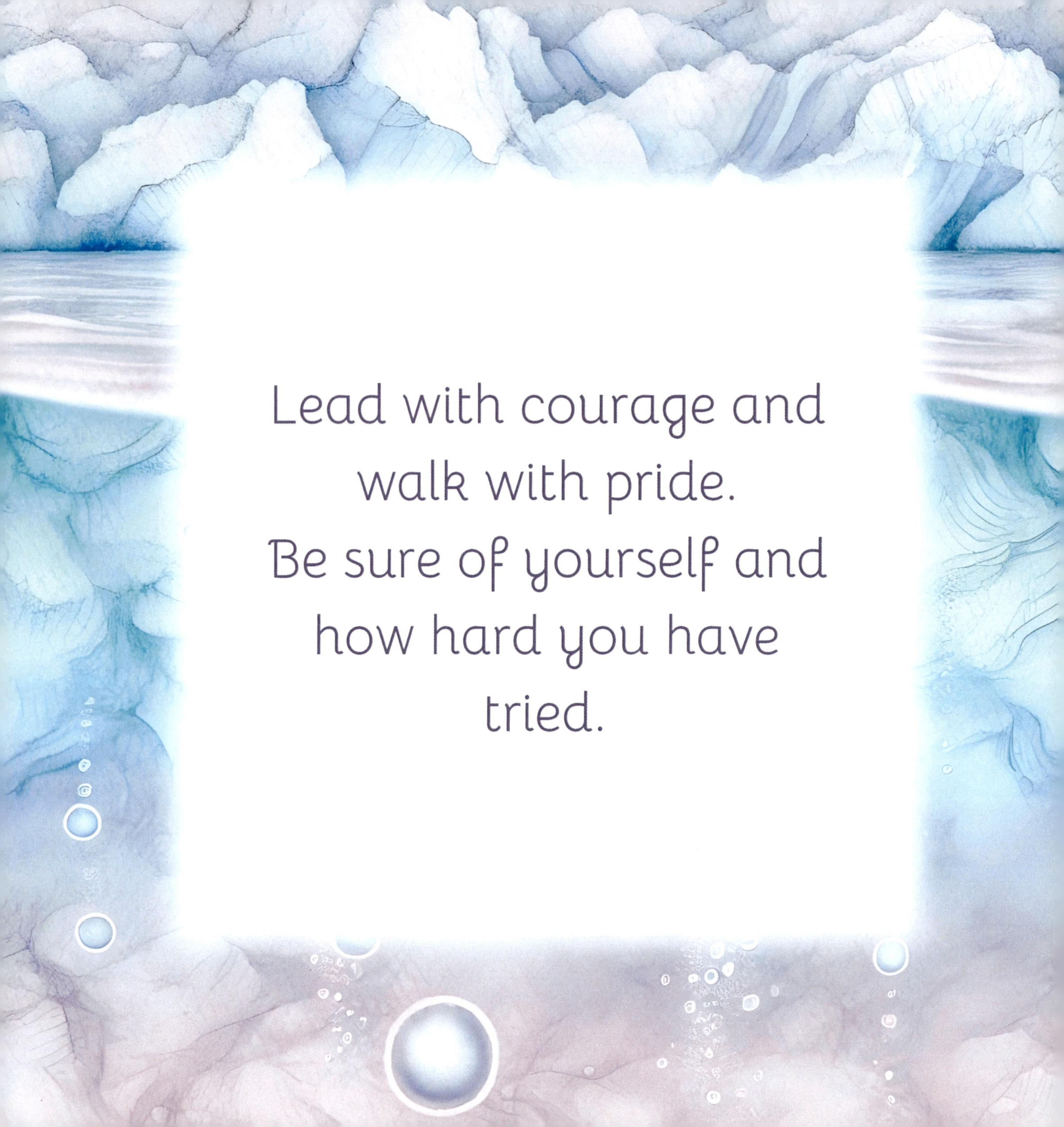

Lead with courage and
walk with pride.
Be sure of yourself and
how hard you have
tried.

Hold family close,
cherish all their love.
It's a gift from God
sent from above.

Be true to yourself in
all that you do.
Always let your true
colors shine through.

So walk with pride and
speak with grace.
For life is a journey, not a race.
In moments of doubt,
look up, not down
The light God carries
can always be found.
With faith and belief,
there's nothing you'll lack.
And know, my dear godchild, I
always have your back.

Made in the USA
Monee, IL
20 August 2025